Investing

The Step By Step Guide To Getting Started With Investing In Short Term Rentals, Making Money Off Of Your First Property, And Formulating A Plan To Generate Additional Monthly Income Right Away

Nelson Erickson

TABLE OF CONTENT

How To Put An End To Your Financial Struggles 1

Things To Think About Before Making A Financial Investment In The Metaverse 20

Monetary Value. Since Then, Various Other Cryptographic Types Of Currency Have Been Developed. 33

The Judge Who Extorts People 51

The Step-By-Step Guide To Failure 60

Distribution Of Assets..84

Gaining An Understanding Of The Pricing Of Options..97

The Metaverse As Well As Crypto 112

Making Money In The Metaverse And How To Do It 124

Make Sure The Storage Is Done Right 167

New Viewpoints That Will Completely Change The Way You Think The Third The Influence That Passive Income Can Have 180

How To Put An End To Your Financial Struggles

Start a budget so you can control your spending. If you have no idea where your money is going or how much you want to put towards your bills, it will be tough to manage your finances in an effective manner.

Spend less money. Recognise the areas in which you are spending more money than necessary. Assuming you are able to cut back on spending on products that aren't necessary, you will have more money available to put towards more important endeavours, such as meeting your financial obligations and putting money away for the future.

Put some money away in case an emergency arises. It can help you reclaim control while also allowing you to avoid incurring any additional financial strain. Because unexpected problems might arise at any time, you should try to have at least three to one and a half years' worth of savings set up for emergencies.

Put an end to creating additional obligations. Taking care of what you owe can free up a significant amount of money, which you can then put towards other endeavours if you so want.

Make some extra money on the side. There are no limits placed on the amount of additional cash that you can acquire. This surplus cash could be put towards the settlement of obligations, the establishment of reserve funds, or the payment of important expenses.

You'll be financially independent in ten years.

You are likely already familiar with some of the fundamentals of investing in income-producing real estate; however, if you are anything like me, you are probably curious in the ways in which this type of investment might affect your life. For a significant portion of us, the pinnacle goal is to amass a lot of wealth and financial success, and this is true for many of us. How exactly do you plan to materially improve your situation, or possibly become wealthy, during the next ten years? In spite of the fact that 10 delves into a variety of strategies for making money from real estate, here is an easy method that will help you become a real estate magnate in fewer than ten years.

The following graph depicts the purchase of four different properties in the northern region over a period of ten years.

In the year 1, Property 1 was purchased for the sum of $300,000.

In the year 3, the amount of $330,000 was paid to acquire property 2. It was acquired by taking money out of the sale of property 1, either through renegotiation or the use of a value advance. In the year 5, a total of $350,000 was spent on the acquisition of properties 3 and 4. They were purchased with the money that was taken from properties 1 and 2.

If you purchased real estate in desirable neighbourhoods and that real estate appreciated at a rate of 6.5% per year, then by the end of the tenth year, you would have amassed a fortune. this appreciation rates may be high for particular locations, but several locations across the United States have consistently seen appreciation at rates that are higher than this.

The chart assumes that your underlying speculation was $30,000 and that each property was purchased with a 10% down payment, received a value credit on a current property, and had a home loan that was amortised over more than 30 years. In addition, the table assumes that each property had a value credit on a current property.

In addition, it is generally acknowledged that each property generates an income of $500 each and every month. This would not be reasonable in the first few decades of ownership of the property; however, once you have owned the property for some time, you will continue to raise rents, and this effectively might be to your profit. In following years, you will make a large amount of money in addition to this. This is something that can be accomplished with relative ease if you invest in multifamily dwellings, such as fourplexes, as will be discussed further on in this book. Using the figure below, it is easy to see that after ten years you will have more than one million dollars in your bank account.

To provide an extra explanation of the benefits of contributing land, let's pause for one minute as an afterthought with a personal computer and compare this to the investment of thirty thousand dollars in the financial market. You would also have one million dollars after 46 years of investing and earning an average of 8% annually. I can't speak for you, but I don't see the point of taking 46 years to accomplish something that can be done in ten.

It Is a Myth That You Have to Use a Hammer

Swinging sledges was an idea that sprang to mind whenever I

contemplated making a contribution to the land. Despite the fact that I had at one time thought about repairing latrines, I ultimately decided that swinging mallets would be a better use of my time because it seemed to be where the real money was. I reasoned that I would need to look for a property that was in distress, fix it up, and then sell it. Isn't that the typical action taken on land? Evidently, this is the case. In addition to this, when all aspects are taken into consideration, it is a fantastic way to bring in money. But what I didn't realise at the time was that flipping houses and making money off of real estate investments is by no means the only way to do either of those things.

It seems to be really complicated, which is perhaps why so many people are unsure about whether or not they should put their money into land. Is that so? It's possible that this isn't the reason you've been waiting, but it was absolutely the reason I resisted for such a significant amount of time. All I kept hearing was "track down persuaded venders, arrange bargains, recover a property, track down inhabitants, and be a landowner." I couldn't believe how much information I was taking in. Because of this, every time I heard the slogan (which I had made up), I felt the desire to throw up a little bit in my mouth. I don't want to make this sound overly dramatic in relation to it. In all honesty, I did not have the slightest bit of interest in engaging in even the most unusual activity. However, if that were the only option to invest in real estate, I think I would have gone ahead and done it. Although the aforementioned activities have the potential to yield significant profits, they are not the sole means by which one might generate income from land investments. If you try to accomplish those things and they don't work out easily for you, or if you hate them, swimming upstream won't help you for benefits that aren't too far off in the future. Even if you succeed in achieving your goal in the end, it might not be worth it if you have to sacrifice your mental health in order to get there.

It is not necessary to use a mallet to plant resources in the soil because there are many different methods available. Investing money in land notes or land speculation trusts (also known as REITs) is the most important approach to take. These strategies are quite similar to investing money in stocks; all you have to do is acquire the note or put money into the trust, and after that, you are normally uninvolved in the process. Another method to acquire real estate is to follow in my footsteps and buy lease-ready or turnkey investment properties. Then, hire a property administrator to take care of the management of the property on your behalf. In this way, you will have real estate. The property has been rehabilitated, and it is either ready to be rented out or is already being rented out. Then, rather than acting in the role of landlord yourself, you hire a property manager to take care of the responsibilities associated with the property on your behalf. After that point, the most of your duties will consist of keeping an eye on the building and the director to make certain that they are operating efficiently and putting certain enhancements into action in the event that they are not. This method is not completely out of the realm of possibility, but it is unquestionably on a lower difficulty level than locating motivated sellers, negotiating deals, rehabilitating properties, locating tenants, and acting as a landlord.

In the realm of land, there is, in all actuality, the possibility for pretty much every conceivable degree of responsibility. Depending on the approach that you take, you may decide how much work you want to put in or how little work you want to put in. The important thing is to look for a strategy that is tailored specifically to your needs and goals. The process of determining which approach this pertains to can take some time.

You could start your research by looking into the following:

Study the various approaches to real estate investment presented in literature.

Attend seminars that cover a variety of investment methods for real estate.

Develop your professional network by interacting with a variety of people working in the sector, and inquire further about the specific strategies utilised by those individuals.

Pay a visit to any online real estate investing forums and pay attention to what other people have to say about the various tactics. Keep in mind that anyone can say whatever they want online, so be wary of those who could sound like they know what they're talking about but in reality might not.

Although this book does not focus in any way on the complexity of each and every land speculation strategy that is currently available, you should be aware that you really do want to examine them in order to choose the method that is most suitable for you. The most important thing to keep in mind is that there are options besides using swinging mallets. When you begin your investigation, it won't be long before you observe your direction to the method of speculation that is suitable for you. This won't take very long at all.

Arbitrage in Rental Prices

The objective of rental arbitrage is to generate passive income by capitalising on the financial potential of the properties owned by other people. Because you will actually be providing value to the owner and even paying them more if necessary, this does not constitute trespassing on their land or stealing their property in any way. You should also make it clear that you will not simply rent the properties without first informing the tenants that you would be listing them on Airbnb. The following are the steps that will lead to a successful rental arbitrage:

Looking for rental property, which might be either a home or a flat depending on your needs. You can find suitable properties to rent out on Airbnb by driving around in certain regions that you have determined to be desirable areas or neighbourhoods and hunting for rentals, which entails looking for properties that have a "FOR RENT" sign.

This is a good technique to find properties to rent out on Airbnb. The goal here is to speak with the owner of the property; if you start calling other phone lines, such as those associated with the property management, it will be far more difficult to do so. One more way to seek for real estate is online, specifically on Facebook marketplace, Craigslist, and by performing a standard search on Google. You should make every effort to avoid getting involved with the property management company. You'll need a lot of experience in negotiating with landlords and persuading them, but if you go directly to Property Management, you'll receive a lot of NOs while you're looking for a YES. You should start with the landlords themselves.

You need to make sure that the rental property is located in a desirable area in order to pre-qualify it. You are able to determine the costs associated with the property as well as compare it to the prices of other Airbnbs in the neighbourhood to get an idea of how much competition there is. If you believe that it meets the requirements, then you can go to the next stage.

Make arrangements to speak with the landlord: Now we've reached the challenging and perhaps nerve-wracking stage of the rental arbitrage process. If you want to rent a property, seek for one that has a sign that says "FOR RENT" either on the door or on the property itself, phone the number shown on the sign, and then make sure you get in touch with the owner of the property. Sometimes the assistant or another person will be the one to answer, but you will need to make sure that you speak with the property owner either over the phone or in person as soon as possible. Also, make sure that the owners of the house are there whenever the potential buyers are doing a home tour.

A whole section will be devoted to discussing how to present your idea to the landlord, so stay tuned for that.

Ensure that the purchase agreement for the property includes a language that gives you the right to sublease or rent out the house through Airbnb: It is essential that you do this in order to ensure that you have the required support. There is no need for you to be concerned about receiving the clause because you can always request that the clause be written into the contract by the landlord. You also do not need to create your own contract because it is a property, and the owners of the property should have the lease agreement as well as contain any essential terms. Because of this, you do not need to create your own contract. You also have the option of requesting that they consult a legal advisor and instructing them to write a contract for you that includes your support of Airbnb in the property. In certain circumstances, this will prove to be of great use. For instance, in the event that you buy the house and the landlord later decides to evict you for using Airbnb, you have the option of pointing out to them that the terms of your rental agreement specify that you are permitted to use the service.

Therefore, those are the processes involved in renting out a house and putting it on Airbnb when you do not own the property yourself. Since we've already gone over the seemingly easy parts, let's move on to the challenging phase, which is pitching the idea to the landlord.

Things To Think About Before Making A Financial Investment In The Metaverse

The concept of the Metaverse is quickly gaining popularity and making an impact on general awareness as a result of Facebook's recent redesign, which has led to additional companies adopting the ecosystem. In recent years, a number of currencies and equities tied to the metaverse have gained momentum as a result of increased attention. Investors regard this increased attention as having potential.

But when it comes to investing in the digital world, what do the majority of investors take into consideration?

An Emerging Market Worth Multiple Billions of Dollars

According to Coingecko, MANA, which has a valuation that is greater than six billion dollars, has been on an ascending monthly trend, gaining by 249.2 percent in the most recent month. The entire market capitalization of the Metaverse currently stands at $36.7 billion.

Grayscale established the Decentraland Trust in February with the intention of investing wholly and passively in MANA. This will allow shareholders to enjoy access to MANA through security while also avoiding the challenges associated with buying, holding, and protecting MANA directly.

Playing games in order to gain tokens for other games is, in Maximo's opinion, another fascinating idea.

This idea appeals to players who would like to own something of value as a result of the time they spend playing a game and has gained a lot of traction in developing nations like Venezuela and the Philippines. These gamers are able to generate a greater salary from playing these games than they could from working conventional jobs or even government jobs.

The ongoing shift in the revenue brought in by game developers is a crucial aspect that is contributing to this upward trend. Earnings from the digital space industry are projected to increase to $390 billion in 2025, up from $180 billion in 2021.

Several different analysts are of the opinion that this pattern is becoming more prevalent. Without initially gaining an understanding of Decentraland and Axie Infinity, prospective investors won't be able to successfully enter the virtual world.

Axie was the first play-to-earn game that was actually popular, while Decentraland has been seriously focused on the Metaverse for decades and specialises in digital property investing. Axie was the first game of its kind.

AXS, which is Axie's token, is the most important asset and now has a market value of $8.88 billion. Over the course of the previous year, it has gone up by 31,211 percent.

Another new venture that is definitely something to look into is UFO Gaming. Its ultimate goal is to create a massive Metaverse that combines the best features of both Decentraland and Axie into a single environment.

UFO intends to become the metaverse universe, if you will, with all of the Metaverse's game, economic, and social components operating on the very same infrastructure. This is in contrast to Decentraland and Axie, which may be thought of as separate galaxies.

Within the past month, the value of UFO on the market has increased by 138.8%, reaching $1.2 billion.

What You Should Watch Out For...

It is "difficult to tell" what criteria speculators need to concentrate on for metaverse-based currencies because the majority of tokens in the gaming industry and the Metaverse are not in the first one hundred.

It is still early; as a result, investors should concentrate on traditional metrics such as market capitalization, protocol revenue, transaction count, and volume. However, the most intelligent way to approach it is from a thematic viewpoint, wagering on whether technology or a particular game will catch up.

The number of users and the frequency with which they take part in the activity can be deduced from the number of transactions as well as the income generated by the protocol. These numbers enable us to understand the trading volume and market capitalization of the assets that are associated with the initiatives. Additionally, they provide insight into the potential movement of the coin.When dealing with matters of this nature, you should engage in extensive investigation. "Because the industry as a whole is still in its infancy, the majority of the enterprises operate in a market that is worth less than a billion dollars, and their behaviour is very unexpected; hence, a great number of studies are required.

Sandbox and Axie Infinity both give off the impression of being feasible efforts in light of market valuation, community growth, and marketing strategies.

Community expansion is an essential factor for shareholders to take into account in the video game industry, but it can be difficult to track.The performance of the game on social media, notably Twitter and YouTube, which are platforms where players engage with content providers and game developers, is the simplest approach to evaluate how well the game is doing. In terms of community growth, "a really fantastic job" is being done by Decentraland because to the fact that it is supporting Creator Contests to encourage its community to generate content for Decentraland. Live streaming and playing games are two of the most important ways to bring in new players.

An uncharted territory in the realm of music

After the success of the virtual concerts created on Fortnite and Roblox, which featured the musicians portrayed as avatars and were viewed by millions of fans all over the world, motion capture technologies have opened the door to further market niches by combining the record world and the live music industry.

Artists and record labels have worked together with Snapchat's Lens Studio and Facebook's Spark AR Studio to develop augmented reality events. TikTok also has its sights set on the augmented reality (AR) market, and the company is hard at work developing innovative tools in order to compete with other companies in the space. According to recent data from App Annie, the amount of time spent by fans on TikTok has recently overtaken the amount of time spent by fans on YouTube in the United States and the United Kingdom. Short form video is the part of the music industry that is growing at the fastest rate.

TikTok is reportedly hard at work on a website that will be known as Effect House, as reported by TechCrunch. There is a lack of information now available, but it appears to be features similar to those found in other social apps. Developers will be able to build augmented reality "effects" for users to incorporate into their own TikTok movies.

As the Chief Executive Officer of Universal Music, Lucian Grainge, stated in interviews that were published before to the record business going public, the music industry is also looking beyond streaming: "The wave of innovation is happening on a variety of platforms, some of which were not even on the radar just a few years ago."

All of these companies are dedicated to finding new technical opportunities that will increase consumption and provide new avenues for musicians to make a profit from the usage of their musical output.

There are certainly more people who interact with music, and they do so in ways that have never been seen before in the history of the music industry. This is because there are new artists, music trends, and ways to discover music, including catalogue music. In addition, there has been an increased penetration of digital music services, mobile devices, expansion of music services into new markets, and new music-based enabling technologies.

It's possible that we haven't been paying attention, but music is present in the majority of our day-to-day activities. Everything from connected cars to health applications, video games, smart speakers, and podcasts is becoming more technologically advanced.

All of this has resulted in the establishment of a large number of start-up companies that operate inside the music industry and develop innovations to incorporate music consumption into ancillary business models.

As we have seen, the world of live streaming is significantly touched by technologies such as VR and AI and will be even more so after the pandemic. Additionally, gaming has now unquestionably penetrated the realm of music, as fans of video games are among the most avid consumers of popular musical genres like hip-hop and rap.

Monetary Value. Since Then, Various Other Cryptographic Types Of Currency Have Been Developed.

Only via the use of cryptographic methods can ownership of cryptographic money units be established.

Alternate digital currencies, also known as altcoins, are a broader category that includes tokens, digital currencies, and several other types of computerised resources that are distinct from bitcoin.

Many alternative cryptocurrencies present basic differences from bitcoin. Ethereum has the most amazing following of any alternative cryptocurrency and is the blockchain that is used the most efficiently all over the world.

A blockchain is a continuously growing list of documents, which are referred to as blocks, that are linked and obtained through the use of encryption.

The information contained in blockchains is designed to be unchangeable under any circumstances. Every single digital currency's coins receive their legitimacy from a distributed ledger called a blockchain. The vast majority of cryptographic currencies are designed to limit the total amount of money that can ever be in circulation at any given time by putting a gradual limit on the amount of new money that can ever be generated.

The digital currency stored within a wallet is not associated with specific individuals but rather with a minimum of one explicit key.

Bitcoin owners are anonymous, but the public ledger, or blockchain, contains a record of every transaction made with the cryptocurrency.

The vast majority of cryptocurrency transactions take place online, outside of traditional financial and administrative institutions. Cryptocurrencies arc also known as digital currencies.

A customer has the ability, through the use of cryptocurrency exchanges, to trade digital forms of money for other resources, such as cash at the standard level, or to trade between multiple computerised currencies.

ATMs that deal in cryptocurrencies are already available, and more of them are continually being developed. It is possible to use a card such as a charge or Visa to withdraw cash and pay for anything you buy, however this feature is not widely available just yet.

It has been argued that the lack of rules governing cryptocurrency networks gives lawbreakers the ability to circumvent obligations and launder money. This argument has been criticised.

The transactions that take place as a result of the utilisation and trading of these alternative cryptocurrencies are outside of traditional financial structures, which can make it easier to evade taxes.

Bitcoin is one of the most prominent cryptocurrencies currently available. The one that is most widely known.Initially implemented in 2009 after having been developed in 2008.

- Ethereum, which is sometimes abbreviated as ETH. It features a decentralised programming stage that allows for the fabrication and execution of applications. The purpose of Ethereum is to create a decentralised system of monetary products that anybody on the earth can have free access to regardless of identification, nationality, or confidence. This is the goal of Ethereum. Customers are able to exchange a form of virtual currency known as ether on the Ethereum platform, which is a product based on the blockchain technology. At the moment, it is the second most significant form of advanced currency after Bitcoin.

• Litecoin, which is often abbreviated as LTC. It has a faster block age rate than Bitcoin does, and as a result, it offers a quicker confirmation time for exchanges. There is a growing number of retailers who are beginning to accept Litecoin as payment.

• Cardano, also known as ADA in some circles. Still in the earliest stages of development. Through the development of decentralised monetary goods, it intends to become the monetary system that governs the entire planet.

• BitcoinCash, abbreviated as BCH when not in use. It is able to handle transactions at a faster rate than the Bitcoinorganisation. There are fewer instances of holding up, and the associated handling fees are reduced.

• Outstanding. In addition, you should be familiar with XLM. Designed to facilitate large-scale transactions between various financial institutions. Huge transactions between banks and venture capital firms, which would typically take a few days and cost a truckload of cash, should now be able to take place virtually immediately without the involvement of any mediators and at a cost that is almost negligible for the parties involved in the transaction. There are currently no restrictions on who can use this open blockchain. The system takes into account any cross-line exchanges that may take place between different monetary standards. The company anticipates that customers will have Lumens in their possession in order to have the choice to operate on the network.

• Binance Coin, abbreviated as BNB when not in use. It is a platform where customers may exchange financial coins and use BNB to convert various types of digital money from one to another.

• Tether, also known as USDT in some circles. Fixing a coin's reasonably anticipated value to a fiat currency or some other external reference in order to reduce its volatility is an essential component of a collection of stable coins. It makes an effort to standardise price differences in order to attract customers who may in some manner be price conscious. The price of Tie is directly proportional to the value of the United States Dollar.

• Monero, which is often referred to as XMR. It is a currency that is secure, confidential, and impossible to track.

Before you add cryptocurrencies to your portfolio, you need first do some research. Cryptocurrencies are fraught with danger.

Putting money into various forms of digital currency is an extremely theoretical endeavour. This market is extremely volatile, and there is a real possibility that significant losses will be incurred.

RIPPLE, THE FOURTH

R

Ipple, also known as XRP, is a cryptocurrency that has been in existence since 2013, and it, along with

Ethereum, appears to be trying to challenge Bitcoin's dominance in the market. The Ripple listing, just like all other digital currencies that belong to the same family, is not based on any kind of tangible cash but rather originates from the internet.

In point of fact, this name refers to both the currency (XRP) and the organisation where it is used, and as such, the meaning of Ripple will become more transparent in the following lines.

It is precisely the recent solid vacillations in Bitcoin's price that bring the topic of virtual monetary standards back to the forefront of conversation. The assembly of Bitcoin, which has already drove the price of the cryptocurrency to over 30,000 dollars, has driven financial backers to check out digital forms of money with another thirst and has thus driven them to question themselves what Ripple is, how it works, and what are its merits and drawbacks. The competing digital currency to Bitcoin is called Ripple, and this is a comprehensive overview of it.

As has been said and referred to previously Ripple, often known as XRP, is a form of virtual currency that does not have a physical counterpart but rather originates on the internet. OpenCoin, which was founded by Chris Larsen and Jed McCaleb, is credited with developing the protocol that underpins the virtual currency, which has been in circulation since around 2013.

According to its creators, the purpose of Ripple is to eliminate and triumph over the obstacles and shortcomings of

Bitcoin. As a result, in the following sections, we will endeavour to highlight each and every difference that exists between the two virtual currencies.

Ripple is based on the concept of the peer-to-peer, or P2P, monetary system. This system intends to eliminate or, at the very least, significantly reduce the costs of intermediation that are associated with financial transactions (costs that may result, for instance, from the intermediation of a bank or a credit).

Ripple operates on a decentralised platform and an open source organisation, just like Bitcoin does. This means that the developers reserve the option to continually mediate and alter as required by the legislation on the use of virtual currency. Ripple is quite similar to Bitcoin in this regard. As a general rule, let us remember by and by how the word Ripple refers to both digital currency and the entire organisation in which it is used to do its business.

The presence of call logs known as Ledger on the Ripple network, on the other hand, is something that cannot be followed in Bitcoin. These logs make it possible to monitor trades and finish transactions in a matter of a few moments. This is something that cannot be done with Bitcoin. One other distinguishing feature of the Ripple network is the capability to trade and move funds without regard to the structure of the receiving or sending currency. For example, I can send dollars to a beneficiary who would prefer to receive euros.

The Ripple network is comprised of three components: a stock exchange, a payments organisation, and the same currency (XRP) that we have been discussing up until this point. However, how exactly does this system function? We might think of Ripple and its organisation as a more modern form of the current arrangement of monetary go-betweens, given that a significant portion of its activity is predicated on trust; nevertheless, before we go any further, let's try to shed some light on the topic by providing an example.

" B and C make the decision to embark on a trip, and each brings a friend along with them. B is the driver for An, and C is in charge of D. While A is only familiar with B, D is only aware of C. Imagine for a moment that An and D, who were previously unknown to you, decide to get a cup of coffee together, but D does not have the money to pay for it. Subject A will be responsible for paying for both, and Subject D will make a proposal to take care of it using Ripple. Therefore, D will stray into the red with C (his partner who will consequently know he will see the cash once more), who will consequently stray into the red with B (the component is always something extremely similar). At long last, B is going to hand over the cash for the espresso to his friend A.Because of this, the operation of the Ripple network is predicated on a mechanism of trust that is represented by IOU credits (I Owe You), which stand in for real currencies. What you give and receive are these credits, which, when processed through one of the so-called Ripple gateways, are turned into actual currency. The most important thing is to recognise that all transactions involving debts, which means that a connection has been made that cannot be broken, take place only between people who have a level of trust in one another. Transactions using Ripple are instant, as well as free.

At the end of the day, XRP is the primary form of currency that circulates within the Ripple organisation. Additionally, it serves as the measurement standard for the purchase and sale of IOU credits. Which means that presuming I need to transport Dollars but only have Euros, the beneficiary of the exchange will purchase my IOUs in Euros for a tonne of Ripple, and sell IOUs in Yen for a handful of extra Ripples. This is because Ripple is a decentralised digital currency that is based on the concept of a distributed ledger. So, this is how the organisation, as well as the structure for digital currency, functions.

As was previously mentioned, the Ripple currency, also known as XRP, is only and exclusively usable within the Ripple organisation and framework itself. It was created there, and it continues to function there. The value of the virtual currency may be broken down into six decimals, and the smallest unit is referred to as a Drop. One million drops are equal to one Ripple.

Ripples, in contrast to Bitcoin, which can produce no more than 21 million units, have already been successfully produced up to the maximum amount of 100 billion, and they are appropriated solely by OneCoin rather than being mined, as is the case with Bitcoin.

The Judge Who Extorts People

Jim anticipated that the completion of the development he had planned would need the purchase of a few properties that were adjacent to one another. He meticulously established buy contracts with each of the land owners, and he continued to carry out the necessary due diligence on each of them. Jim started making plans for the closings on each of the properties once it was determined that the investigations and examinations had produced satisfactory results.

The back eight parts of land that belonged to a neighbourhood judge were the primary parcel that was sold. Jim got in touch with each vendor to organise the conclusion, and while he was having a conversation with the adjudicator, the men of honour asked him to bring the event to a halt immediately. Jim's natural inquisitiveness led him to inquire as to the rationale behind the necessity of closing after all of the other landowners. The authority that had been assigned to respond stated, "As an adjudicator, I have managed a large number of cases, some of which involved dishonest business experts and financial backers." I don't care whether you think I'm cynical or just plain mistrustful; the fact is that I have to find a way to terminate my ordeal if you have anything available. Jim shrugged his shoulders and then gave his assent to the request made by the constituted authorities.

After closing on and purchasing all of the other properties, it was finally time to close on the adjudicator's 8 separate portions of land. Jim was in for a rude awakening when the chosen authority informed him that he would simply have to close the business in the event that he received an additional $250,000 in funds. In response, Jim asked, "Would you say that I am crazy?" We have an agreement that is legally binding on all of us. This is an attempt at blackmail. I shall sue for the direct carrying out of the sentence if you do not withdraw it and you are aware that I will prevail. In response to this, the designated authority responded in a calm and collected manner by saying, "When you get that triumph through the equity framework, it will be quite a while not too far off." I am fully aware of the steps that need to be taken to ensure that this matter is put off till a great many years from now. During this time, you would have been required to administer the local fees and obligations for such a large number of distinct properties. This task would have taken a significant amount of time. In addition, at that moment, the market might be completely different, your targeted residents might no longer be interested, and this development might end up being a total bust. It would be far more cost effective in the long run to pay me an additional $250,000 than to pursue the alternative.

Jim reluctantly agreed, and then he handed the adjudicator an additional two hundred and fifty thousand dollars in cash.

The Formula for Economic Independence

I came to the conclusion that, in light of my circumstances, I needed to press on with my life at an early age. I had the thought that my parents were always there for both my sister and I, and I want to be able to provide that same kind of support for my own children the way that they have always done. Even though both of my parents worked full-time jobs, they were fortunate enough to have careers that gave them some leeway in their schedules. My mother had the good fortune to work for an organisation that allowed her to adjust her schedule on a case-by-case basis, and my father was self-employed, so he was able to choose his own hours. This gave them both the flexibility they needed in their schedules. After taking into account the situations of both of my parents, I came to the conclusion that being a business visionary was the most reliable way to realise my ambition of achieving financial independence.

I pursued a few different endeavours throughout the course of the subsequent twenty years until I finally arrived on land. During this excursion, I was well aware that all I was doing was getting me closer and closer to my goal. I had no idea how much information I would gather in relation to the number of diverse women who were working towards the same objective as I was.

Putting Things in Context

My entire life, I have spent a disproportionate amount of time in the company of males relative to females. My sibling's coworkers from the various organisations he played on frequently stopped by our house. I attended a school that was once exclusively for young men, where the male students outnumbered the female students by a ratio of three to one, and when I was in school, I lived in a house with 14 other young men. I know, right? That's insane, right? Dcspite this, I felt more comfortable being around young males than I was around young women when I was their age. I liked the way in which they thought, I admired the ease with which they overcame obstacles, and I favoured the opportunities that inexplicably seemed to be directed in their favour. To tell the truth, being around young males was far less difficult than being around young girls.

For the past 10 years, I have immersed myself in the country, and despite the fact that I did not first recogniseit, I have ultimately found myself to be primarily surrounded by men. I find myself at gatherings, tables, and events where guys dominate the space, both in terms of appearance and in terms of their physical presence, on a regular basis, and I continue to do so right up until the present day.

The "Aha!" Moment

In the early spring of 2018, I went to a land conference that lasted for multiple days. During one of the breaks, I was approached along with every other women who was participating to sit together during one of the snacks. Liz Faircloth and AndresaGuidelli, who are also co-founders of The Real Estate InvestHer, were the ones who initially initiated this solicitation. There were more than 450 people present at that meeting, but there were less than 20 women who were seated at the table, which is less than 5% of the total participants. During the time that everyone was getting to know one another, I was amazed to see that we were able to fit all of us at only two tables that were pushed together. It was at that point in time when I became aware, for the first time, that there were only a few ladies present.

The Step-By-Step Guide To Failure

We have effectively covered how to ease your transition into land investing through the use of techniques such as honing in on your attributes, adhering to what works out easily for you, and being strategic in determining which land investing course may be the ideal fit for your goals. But what about the final piece of the puzzle that is your mindset? What exactly do you need to do in order to be successful?

Stopping for a moment to think about what you are not going to do is one of the simplest ways to figure out what it will take for you to be successful. If you can avoid the associated gaffes, there is a far better chance that you will get at your destination, and hopefully with lessheadaches along the way. This is assuming, of course, that you will be able to avoid the gaffes.

Investing with a minimal amount of education under your belt is a mistake.

There is a reason why an adult is always there and floaties are never given to a young child to play in the water alone. They would die of asphyxiation. You will essentially die of asphyxiation if you jump into land contributing without having taken any swim examples beforehand. In addition, if you take just one swimming instruction, you won't be able to learn how to swim.

 In point of fact, similar to the majority of things that occur throughout regular life, the one who does not rush will win the race. It is of utmost importance to acquire training in land investing, given the scope and significance of this field. Putting up the effort to learn some fundamental information and add it to your toolkit is a fundamental requirement. In the event that you do not develop a solid foundation, you could put everything at risk by investing it in something that is completely unreliable.

To become familiar with the fundamentals does not call for any kind of financial investment. You should never allow yourself to become so hurried that you miss out on the opportunity to gain fundamental knowledge.

To be in every way more prepared and to make more risk-free endeavours, all that is required is a modest amount of education. If I were to choose only a few of the most fundamental aspects of land investment that any potential backer absolutely has to be aware of, they would be as follows:

contrasts between various techniques for investing, as well as how each strategy connects to a specific set of goals

risks posed by each approach, as well as suggestions for mitigating those dangers

how to calculate the results

analysis of the market and the city

This is a very brief summary that may be modified in a reasonable amount of time. If you put in the time and effort to become familiar with each of these four things, you will have put yourself light years ahead of the vast majority of people who are participating in land contributing, and you will likely achieve success much more quickly in the future. It doesn't mean that you won't ever fail, but it does indicate that the chances of you doing so are getting lower, which means that the level of failure is getting lower as well.

Antiquities and other valuable collectibles

Due to the fact that they are not affected by growth rates or the stock market, speculating with antiques and collectibles typically results in a higher return.

The value of collections and collectibles does not fluctuate; rather, it increases in direct proportion to the rarity and quality of the item being collected.

They have the potential to deliver extraordinary profits over a longer period of time. You should seek the recommendations of professionals or cultivate a broad knowledge base.

Clocks, currencies, cameras, comic books, stamps, bourbon, and load up games are just few of the collectibles that are considered to be among the most valuable and valuable collectibles.

According to the website sammydvintage.com, a Pinner Qing Dynasty container has a value of $80.2 million. This makes it one of the most valuable collectibles in the world.

The first step in differentiating and appreciating collectibles and collectibles is frequently determining the thing's creator by looking for an imprint or signature on the item. This can be a time-consuming process.

When it comes to identifying historic furniture, one of the most important things to look at is the era in which it was made.

The original thing was changed as little as possible, which drives up the value of the finished product.

Old fashioned sales is an excellent place to go if you need to get collectibles valued since they have experienced valuers, and as long as you carry the object with you or provide images, they will typically offer you a free valuation with the assumption that you will sell your things through them. If you need to get collectibles valued, you should go there.

 The age of an item is what differentiates it as collectible, vintage, or both. Things that are considered antique typically have a minimum age of one hundred years.

Advantages include the following: • You can invest in anything • Even the most unusual things increase in value over the longer term • They are tangible • They can be transported easily • Global investments • Gain capital worth over the rate of regular inflation • You can participate in your investment

• The antique market is not regulated • If you really want to recover the money restricted in your speculation, there is no guarantee they will sell at the costs you want • They can be amazingly expensive • The antique industry is volatile • It is expensive to keep, keep up with, and store antiques

You can find collectibles and collectibles in stores, on the internet, and even in trades. Bartering is another option. You are able to sell them via the internet.

PARTNER IS THE FOURTH STEP

NOW THAT YOU HAVE A VERY DETAILED PLAN, A COMPREHENSION OF WHAT YOU ARE GETTING YOURSELF INTO, AND HAVE CHOSEN A REGION TO INVEST IN, ONE OF THE MOST IMPORTANT THINGS THAT EVERY SUCCESSFUL VR FINANCIAL BACKER DOES IS COLLECT THE BEST TEAM THEY CAN FIND IN THE MARKET THEY ARE INVESTING IN. Your success will have a direct correlation to the competence of the professionals you collaborate with. In this field, your professional connections are invaluable, which is why putting together the best team possible should be your first priority right now.

Rentals of excursion vehicles for shorter periods of time are a local business. Working with the appropriate persons makes your life a significant amount simpler as you construct your portfolio of lucrative vacation rentals. Along the way, you will collaborate with a wide variety of specialists from a variety of fields. Realtors, finance subject matter experts, property managers, excursion rental interior architects, assessment and protection professionals to ensure that your organisation is set up in the ideal method, support experts, and cleaners are just some of the several business specialists that are available. The list continues on and on.

We will talk about some of these accomplices and how to find them, but this is by no means a complete breakdown of everyone involved. Your fantasy team will consist of a large number of specialists who are specifically tailored to your needs. Your top three partners—the Realtor, the money, and the board—will serve as wonderful resources for the other members of your team. The reality is that you will have a group of partners who will be essential to your success, and the process of developing that fantasy group is a significant part of the cycle at the present time. For a very long time, Jared and Jamie looked for an opportunity to make an investment in real estate that was suitable to their situation and would allow them to do it profitably. When I first met them, they were in the process of determining whether or not investing money into summer houses was the best course of action for them. As an accountant by trade, Jared is very frameworks and interface oriented due to the nature of his employment. While Jared was looking for the right match, he hadn't found the certainty to move forward on anything until he found our cycle. Prior to that, he hadn't found the right fit for anything. Compared to the extensive variety of options that he was investigating, our outline seemed to be sufficient.

They changed from being completely afraid and worried to being sure and conclusive when Jared and Jamie pulled the trigger and concentrated on what happened after we had interacted with them. In only 22 days, they were able to acquire the knowledge and assurance necessary to go on a trip down to their favourite area to get away, meet with a portion of their fantasy group, locate a great house, make a proposal, and close on an incredible Lifestyle Asset. The fantasy group that we assisted them in constructing was a major contributor to this level of assurance.

Modelling and Analysis of Financial Markets is the topic of 6.

The exchange of assets takes place on the various financial markets. These assets may take the form of equities, bonds, derivatives, commodities, or foreign currency. The market provides a venue for companies to lower the risks associated with raising financing. When it comes to governing assets and the people who trade them, there is always some kind of open system in place. There are many different kinds of financial marketplaces operating online nowadays. These include:

The bourse (stock market)

The market for bonds

The market for commodities

The market for derivatives

The market for foreign exchange

Only one of these categories has been discussed in this book, and that is the stock market. The stock market is made up of a number of different microstructures, each of which includes trading agents and several other participants. These agents are accountable for conducting research on the current market pricing in order to determine the prices and order quantities for each trading period. These agents can be divided into three main categories, which are as follows:

They never deviate from the path set by the market and are known as followers. That is, in order to purchase shares, they wait for prices to increase before doing so. They continue to sell the same stock even when the price drops.

Mean reverters are investors that behave in thc opposite direction of the followers in the market in the expectation that the stock price would eventually move in the way that is favourable to them.

Fundamentalists are those who believe that stock values should be determined only by the information that is available.

Before they will buy or sell shares, they investigate the market to determine if the prices are accurate.

When it comes to the oversight of these markets, both financial modelling and financial analysis are utilised to compile information that is utilised to determine the elements that influence market activity. When modelling the prices of stocks, there are always two methodologies that are employed in common. There is also basic modelling in addition to technical modelling.

Technical modelling focuses on the collection of statistical information on stock prices, but fundamental modelling delves further into the mathematical explanation of stock behaviour, which influences its price. Both types of modelling are used to predict future stock values.

Earning Dividends From Mutual Funds and Exchange Traded Funds is the Topic of 5 of This Book.

In the previous , we went over the importance of having a diversified portfolio. When it comes to making financial investments, each and every financial counsellor that you consult with will stress the significance of maintaining a varied investment portfolio. However, it can be rather challenging for an individual investor to truly diversify their financial portfolio. It is tough to attract enough companies into your portfolio while simultaneously thoroughly examining their fundamentals and maintaining track of them once you have sunk money into them. It is also difficult to evaluate and keep track of the companies once you have invested money in them. Additionally, it is challenging for an individual investor to put enough money into each company to genuinely receive good dividend payments from those companies.

Investing your money in funds that provide dividends is one strategy that can help you navigate around some of these challenges. You might potentially gain exposure to hundreds or even thousands of companies as a result of this. Investing in the suitable funds allows you to gain exposure to a wide variety of markets, giving you the ability to diversify your portfolio.

Without going to the trouble of investing in individual equities, this strategy may be the best option for certain individuals. There are some people who are only interested in investing in individual companies and find the concept of investing in funds to be uninteresting. The power of this notion lies, however, in the fact that a large number of investors are able to combine the two strategies. You could invest in five to ten of your favourite stocks rather than twenty different equities, and then place the rest of your investment capital in a few different dividend paying funds that give you highly diversified exposure. This would be a better use of your money.

What exactly is a mutual fund, then?

A mutual fund is a pool of money that is gathered from investors and used to buy shares of stock or other investments. This money is pooled together rather than kept separate. When it comes to mutual funds, the pool of money that is gathered is then split up into individual shares, which are also frequently referred to as units. After that, the shares are sold to investors, which results in the investors owning a portion of the underlying shares of stock or other assets; nonetheless, the business that manages the fund is the true owner of the securities that underpin the fund.

A mutual fund is going to make investments in a diverse range of assets across the board. Therefore, it might potentially invest in fifty or one hundred different equities, or even more. The S&P 500, the Russell 2000, and the Dow Jones Industrial Average are three of the most common main stock indexes that are followed by many mutual funds. Therefore, a fund that tracked the S&P 500 would have to own shares in each of the 500 firms that are included in the index. In the case of the Russell 2000, the fund would have ownership stakes in all 2000 of the companies that make up the index.

This offers a level of diversification that is just not feasible for the majority of individual investors. As a result, a large quantity of diversification is provided. If you don't have a million dollars lying around, you won't be able to buy shares in any of the firms that are included in the Russell 2000 or the S&P 500. You won't even be able to acquire shares in the 500 companies that are included in the S&P 500.

You can gain access to these varied investments, however, through the use of a mutual fund. Therefore, you are in a position to reap the benefits of large diversification in a manner that protects you from potential financial losses. If the remainder of the economy continued to be stable, the failure of one or two, or even five of the companies that are included on the S&P 500, would not have a significant impact on your situation. On the other hand, if you have such a diverse investment portfolio in significant corporations, you are in a position to make the most of the growth opportunities that the stock market presents. In the following section, we are going to discuss the fact that investments in exchange traded funds and mutual funds both offer the opportunity to receive dividend payments.

Distribution Of Assets

You should make room in your financial portfolio for a new type of security called a government bond.

A bond can be thought of as a type of loan.

When we buy a bond, we are handing over money to the government in exchange for a promise that it would repay us in a certain number of years with interest. This currency is traded on a public exchange just like any other stock, and its value rises and falls according on the demand for it – exactly like the value of an actual stock would. The value of a bond, on the other hand, is notable due to the fact that its volatility is significantly lower than the volatility of publicly listed corporations' shares. The value of stocks is notorious for being highly unpredictable, as it regularly swings between rising and declining prices. On the other hand, it is extremely unusual to hear of a government going bankrupt at the same rate as the private sector. Even if or when something like that occurs, the warning signs are almost always very blatant and loud.

Your bonds in your investment portfolio will fluctuate at a rate that feels more like a train ride across the country, whereas the average annual return on corporate stocks is between 8% and 11%. The annual return on bonds, which is considered to be a safe and reliable investment, is typically between 1% and 3%.

Because there is a lower degree of correlation between the movement of bonds and the movement of stock indices, diversifying an investment portfolio with bonds is a good investment strategy that is recommended by financial experts. Additionally, the anticipated rate of return for either option is positive. Return to the second if you have forgotten what expectation is.

Because active investors typically sell their shares of company stock when the price of those shares is falling and then purchase bonds, the performance of the various markets is frequently inconsistent with one another. Following this, the value of the bond securities goes up, while the value of the shares goes down significantly. The diversification benefits provided by a portfolio that includes both stocks and bonds make it a popular choice among investors. After all, who wouldn't want to take a fall on something that was comfortable?

But as lazy investors, should we be interested in the ups and downs of the market? In no uncertain terms, no. It makes absolutely no difference to us whatsoever. The passive investor does not need to be a scholar in probabilities; however, the word "expectation" still reverberates in our heads. Do you remember when you first started reading this book? Expectations regarding the value of stocks and bonds have remained consistently optimistic throughout history.

Let's look at two different scenarios that could occur:

Portfolio 1 is performing consistently. It is made up of bonds and shares in equal proportions.

The asset allocation of Portfolio 2 is a little bit different from the first because it consists of 80% shares and 20% bonds.

Let's start with a $100,000 investment in just two exchange-traded funds (ETFs):

An exchange-traded fund that has its assets invested in a major US stock index such as the S&P 500.

An exchange-traded fund that invests in general government bonds of the United States, similar to Vanguard's BND securities.

Let's incorporate the following information into the calculation:

In 1990, a $100,000 investment portfolio was first opened for business.

A financial commitment of $1,500 per month through the year 2020.

One final consideration: over the course of 30 years, the investor exercised caution and made it a point to check the portfolio's stability every three months. The following is what it means to have a balanced portfolio:

The investor examines her investment portfolio on a regular basis, for example, once every three months or once every six months, to verify that the proportions of her holdings remain the same as they were on day one. A hint: the ratios will almost certainly shift in the future due to the fact that, as we are well aware, the value of stocks has a greater propensity to increase than the value of bonds.

Therefore, if you invested $10,000 in stock indices and the same amount in bond indices, you shouldn't be surprised if, after a year, the value of the stock portion of the portfolio has increased significantly more than the value of the bond portion. In order for the investor to maintain the same proportion of assets, she will need to sell the securities associated with her stocks and use the proceeds to purchase bonds through those stocks. This will bring the investor's portfolio back to a balance of 50 percent stocks and 50 percent bonds.

For instance, if after a year she discovers that the value of her stock holdings has increased to $10,500 while the value of her bond holdings has increased to $10,100, she may decide to sell $200 worth of stock indices and buy $200 worth of bonds, thereby rebalancing the proportions of her investment portfolio to 50/50:

The value of the shares: $10,300

The cost of bonds is $10,300.

Take a look at the following graph, which demonstrates the evolution of portfolios over time. Don't let the complicated chart throw you off your game. Continue reading. You will be successful. I swear to it.

Portfolio 1, which contains an equal amount of shares and bonds, is a strong contender in the competition for the title of most stable investment portfolio. Only four years out of its entire existence have resulted in a decrease in its value, and the worst of these years resulted in a loss of almost 18% of its value. During its entire existence, it has been around for three decades. The portfolio experienced a loss of value equal to one quarter of its previous level (-25%).

In comparison to this portfolio, the more balanced one known as Portfolio 2

(80/20) went through three decades that were characterised by slightly higher levels of volatility and a total of five negative years, as opposed to only four in Portfolio 1. During that terrible year, it shed nearly thirty percent of its total body mass. I sincerely hope that the people who own this portfolio weren't watching the portfolio when it took its steepest dive because it was a significant one, accounting for 42% of the entire portfolio.

However, if the investors in both portfolios were neither concerned about the declines nor excited by the growth, there is a clear winner, and it is by a large margin: the portfolio with the lower risk.

In the year 2020, Portfolio 1, which was split 50/50, accumulated a total value of $1,433,991 (of which 78% was profit).

In the year 2020, the value of Portfolio 2, which was split 80/20, was calculated to be $1,972,791 (of which 85% was profit!).

Even though both portfolios contained the exact same amount of money, the performance of the equity portfolio was superior to the performance of the more moderate portfolio because the investor was willing to accept greater volatility in exchange for greater profits.

THREE: WHAT DOES IT MEAN TO HAVE A BUDGET?

A method of keeping track of how much money you have and how much money you spend is to create and adhere to a budget. When you are aware of how much things cost and where your money goes, you open the door to many positive experiences.

If you are aware that candy can be purchased at the local drugstore for fifty cents, you will not spend seventy-five cents on a candy machine. In addition, knowing how much money you have to spend can prevent you from spending more than you actually have. When you have a budget, there is less chance that you will run out of money by the middle of the week, forcing you to either ask for more money or forego the things you want.

The advantage of having a budget is that it enables you to buy all of the things that you truly want, which is one of the best things about having a budget. It sheds light on the amount of money that is wasted on things that are neither required nor desired by the individual. Last but not least, a budget enables you to put money aside for expensive items that you simply cannot afford to purchase right now.

Why do some people choose to ignore the existence of budgets?

People have the misconception that budgets are terrible because they require you to give up things that bring you joy in your life. They have the misconception that a budget is similar to going on a diet, in which you are required to deprive yourself of fun activities. In point of fact, the opposite is true. Let's take a look at what transpired after a young man by the name of

Thomas established a budget, as well as the means by which he was able to accomplish everything that he desired.

The financial plan that Stephen has created is outstanding.

Stephen, who was only fourteen at the time, never had enough money. He kept a long list of things that he desired but were out of his reach. As a direct consequence of this, he ran into issues on a regular basis. For instance, he once squandered the money that his father had given him in order to pay for a class trip by purchasing additional chocolates. Following that, he recouped the money for the vacation by selling his favourite baseball card. Stephen was a grouch during the class trip, didn't enjoy the candy, and didn't get the baseball card he wanted. Is there any chance that this young boy can be saved? Yes. Keeping the cost in mind!

The first thing you need to do when making a budget is to record every single source of revenue, regardless of the form the money takes. Included in this total are all labour payments, gifts, and allowances. You shouldn't be concerned about the money that you only find occasionally. That is not something that can be counted on on a weekly basis. When discussing finances, any and all of this cash is referred to as income.

Gaining An Understanding Of The Pricing Of Options

When it comes to successfully trading options, one of the first things you need to do is gain an understanding of how options are given their relative value. This is one of the most important things you can do. In the end, the price is determined by a combination of the anticipated dividends that the underlying stock will generate, the interest rates, the volatility, the time value, the intrinsic value, and the stock price at the time of calculation. Out of these, the volatility, time value, intrinsic value, and current stock price play the largest role in determining what you will pay for the options that you purchase on a minute-to-minute basis.

It is important to understand the difference between any premiums (profits) that the trade might generate and the theoretical value of the option in question when it comes to making a decision as to whether or not a potential option is right for you. This is because the trade might generate premiums. The amount that the buyer will pay to obtain what is specified in the option is referred to as the premium, and the premium also includes the sum of money that the seller will receive once they have written the option. In contrast, the theoretical value of an option is the amount that the option ought to be worth based on all of the current market signs. This value is calculated by taking into account the current state of the market.

The most significant factors

Price of the stock as of right now: Although there is not a perfect one-to-one correlation between them, the current stock price and any related options move in the expected direction when it comes to how they are both affected by each other. In general, the price of calls will increase along with the price of the underlying stock while the price of puts will decrease. However, the situation will be reversed if the price of the underlying stock continues to fall.

Intrinsic Value: The intrinsic value is the amount of value that the underlying stock is guaranteed to keep, even though the time value continues to decrease over time. This is in contrast to the time value, which continues to increase as time passes. You can calculate the "intrinsic value" of a call option in one of two ways: either divide the current price of the underlying stock by the difference between that price and the strike price of the related call option, or use the formula below. On the other hand, the intrinsic value of a put option can be calculated by first deducting the price of the put from the current stock price, then dividing the resulting number by the stock price. This will give you the intrinsic value of the put option.

In either scenario, the outcome will be a reflection of the nature of the benefit that would be generated by carrying out the action in question if the option were exercised. In essence, it can be interpreted as the least amount that you will receive from exercising the option. For instance, if a company's stock is currently trading at approximately $34.80 per share, the intrinsic value of a call option with a strike price of $30 would be calculated to be $4.80 because $34.80-$30 equals $4.80. If this were a put option, then it would have no intrinsic value because $30 minus $34.80 equals -4.80, and the intrinsic value of a put option with a negative value is always 0.

Time Value: The time value of an option refers to the amount of time that remains until the option is exercised, but it can also be thought of more effectively as the probability that the option's total value will be greater than its intrinsic value. Simply taking the price of the option in question and deducting the amount that corresponds to its intrinsic value will get you the answer you need to determine the time value of any option. Expect your options to lose approximately 30 percent of their value in the first 50 percent of their time on the market, with the remaining 70 percent of their value decreasing over the remaining portion of their time on the market. This is a general rule to follow.

If the related contract is about to expire in 30 days and the related call option is currently going for $5, then the time value for the call is going to be set at 20 cents because $5 (the cost of the option) is subtracted from $4.80 (the intrinsic value). This is because the time value for the call is determined by subtracting the cost of the option from the intrinsic value. In the previous example, the company had shares priced at $34.80. If, on the other hand, the same stock was associated with an option that has a current value of $6.85 and was not going to expire for another 9 months, then it would have a time value of $2.05

because \$6.85 minus \$4.80 equals \$2.05. In any event, the intrinsic value does not change, but the remaining portion of the price shifts depending on the time value that is ultimately determined.

The amount of volatility that the stock in question is likely to experience in the time frame that is being given is another factor that has a direct influence on the time value. If it is anticipated that the stock price will not fluctuate much, then the time value cost associated with it will be relatively low. On the other hand, this is not the case for stocks that have a high rate of volatility because there is a significantly increased chance that they will experience a significant shift in value before their expiration date.

Volatility: While it is extremely important to measure correctly, volatility is the most subjective of all of the primary influences, which can make it difficult to do so properly. This is especially the case for new options traders. To our great good fortune, there are a number of calculators that can be used to assist in accurately determining volatility. In addition, there are a lot of different kinds of volatility; however, the types of volatility that you should be most concerned with right now are historical volatility and implied volatility.

The amount of volatility that the underlying stock in question has experienced in the past is referred to as its historical volatility. It sheds light on potential future movements, specifically how significant they are likely to be, which is helpful in predicting the future.

If you take a look at the historical volatility, it will be much simpler for you to determine the appropriate exercise price that you will want to pick. The current state of the market and relevant related prices are used to calculate what is known as "implied volatility," which is the amount of volatility that the underlying stock currently possesses. You can use it to assist you in precisely determining the potential value of a possible business transaction.

The Authoritative Guide to Trading Penny Stocks, Complete with Step-by-Step Instructions

When you read about penny stocks, you put yourself in a more precarious position than if you were actually trading in them. When considering alternative exchanges, such as pink sheets and OTC markets, rather than the more conventional NYSE and NASDAQ, the level of risk increases significantly.

Because of this, it is of the utmost importance to have stringent and significant criteria under which the penny stock will fall, and it is for this reason that you want to practise matters such as risk management.

One possibility worth considering is engaging in the day trading of penny stocks. Penny stocks are much better suited for the short-term game, whereas regular stocks are unquestionably better suited for the long-term game, as you may have seen mentioned multiple times before.

When it comes to trading, one of the most common pieces of advice regarding risk management is to avoid holding onto your stocks overnight, as this is the time when the most damage can be done to your portfolio without your knowledge.

Now, the very first step that you can take with day trading is to trade only the very best and to leave the rest of the market alone. It is a straightforward idea that can be categorised under the principle that one must adhere to stringent standards. You can use a stock scanner, which will make your life a lot simpler and cut the amount of work time you spend figuring out trades by at least half, if not even more.

You can begin each day by listing the stocks that meet the criteria in which you will engage in trading. This can be done first thing in the morning.

The next thing you need to do is make sure you are trading the highest quality setups. Trading with the best stocks is the first step in the process. Now, you need to be able to trade using the most effective setups, such as bull flags or even flat top breakout patterns.

These are the chart patterns that the vast majority of professional traders simply trade. This is due to the fact that they present the lowest level of risk and also share many other characteristics in common. In most cases, both of these patterns require the stock market to make some significant new highs, followed by a brief decline that coincides with a market decline. If you ever find yourself uncertain about something, you should think about inquiring about and finding out whether the stock you are selling has a type of event that happens once a year. Normally, now would be the best time to enter the market and begin trading with this stock. In most cases, a bull flag can be recognised when the candlestick on the sales of trade makes a new high immediately after the pullback has in fact taken place. This is one of the telltale signs of a bull flag.

The following thing you should do is, if at all possible, sign up for a chat room where other traders congregate. If you want to be one of the best traders, it is absolutely helpful to surround yourself with other people who are also among the best. You will be able to pick up quite a bit of knowledge from them, and on top of that, they are part of a welcoming community that will assist you with your problems, trades, and even mental tricks. You shouldn't blindly follow a trader's advice, but if you're just starting out, you should absolutely make it a point to learn as much as you can from those who have spent years perfecting the art of trading. However, before you join a chat room for traders, check to see that it is staffed by experts, and be wary of con artists because online communities are notorious for attracting fake members. However, a significant advantage is the possibility of having a community that tells others about a profession or business that has a great deal of untapped potential. It is much more likely that a profitable trade will be identified, which is an extremely advantageous possibility in its own right. A community not only teaches you from its members but also helps you achieve goals that are congruent with your own, which can result in financial gains that you might not have been able to achieve on your own.

It's possible that, at the end of the day, you'll find the repetitive patterns to be quite boring; however, repetition is often essential in certain situations. The making of a multimillionaire through trading does not require the use of any massive secret ingredients or recipes. However, getting one's education from those who are already successful in their field, modelling one's behaviour after successful strategies, and remaining steadfast to one's commitments almost always result in financial success.

The Metaverse As Well As Crypto

In the past few weeks, an exciting new term known as the metaverse has entered the lingo of the cryptocurrency industry. It's possible that you're scratching your head, trying to figure out what the heck it is and what it means for crypto. In this part, we are going to go into great depth about every little detail and tell you exactly where you can go to find hidden treasures.

The word "metaverse" seems to be popping up virtually everywhere these days. This is primarily due to Mark Zuckerberg, who announced in late October that Facebook would be rebranding to Meta at the Connect 2021 conference. In the announcement, Zuckerberg presented the idea of something similar to a Facebook 2.0. It is a new and alternative model for Facebook that aims to bring the metaverse to life and assist people in connecting with one another, locating communities, and growing businesses. It is in Meta's own words that "the metaverse will feel like a hybrid of today's online social experiences, sometimes expanded into three dimensions or projected into the physical world." You will be able to participate in shared, fully immersive experiences with other people, even if you are unable to be physically present with them, and you will be able to do things together that you are physically incapable of doing in the real world.

As it relates to cryptocurrencies, the rebranding of Facebook to Meta caused a number of NFT and VR-related coins' values to skyrocket in a relatively short amount of time. For example, shortly after the announcement of Meta was made, the value of the native Decentraland token known as MANA increased by more than 400 percent.

It is not an easy task to condense everything that can be said about the metaverse into a single sentence because there are so many different points of view, ways of conceptualising it, and a great number of definitions. A recent presentation given by the Wall Street Journal describes the metaverse as "an extensive online world where people interact via digital avatars." This is a rather broad definition of what the metaverse actually is.

Does this ring a bell?

If you enjoy playing the Sims video games, figuring this out shouldn't be too difficult for you. Despite the fact that this definition offered by the journal encompasses all of the primary and fundamental components of what constitutes the metaverse, it appears to be rather simplistic.

The American author Neil Stevenson came up with the term "metaverse," which is a portmanteau word made up of the words "meta" and "universe." Stevenson first used the term in his science fiction novel "Snow Crash," which was published in 1992. Snow Crash is a novel that was inspired by virtual reality and takes place in a three-dimensional virtual space that is meant to be interpreted as a metaphor for the real world. The novel features humans portrayed as avatars interacting with one another and artificially created software agents.

In the book, the users of Stevenson's metaverse perceive it to be a predominantly urban setting that has been developed along a road with a width of one hundred metres and the name 'The Street.' A pitch-black and flawlessly spherical planet is completely encircled by "the street," which runs its entire length. Users of this metaverse can access it through personal terminals that project a high-definition VR through special goggles worn by the users who experience the metaverse from a first-person perspective.

Another more recent depiction of the metaverse can be found in the science fiction movie "ready player one," which was directed by Steven Spielberg and released in 2018. Both Snow Crash and Ready Player One depict the metaverse in a manner that is analogous to a hypothetical and somewhat futuristic iteration of the internet. The metaverse is presented as a space that is preoccupied primarily with augmented reality and artificial intelligence. A world ravaged by climate change and an unprecedented fossil fuel crisis is depicted in the novel "Ready Player One," and the metaverse serves as a source of solace for the characters.

The concept of the metaverse is expanding at an astoundingly quick rate, not only in terms of increased cultural awareness but also increased financial value. Some industry analysts believe that the metaverse will be the next major investment theme in both the cryptocurrency and traditional technology spaces. This is due to the fact that the concept of a reality centred on a metaverse is gradually but surely starting to become more mainstream.

According to Igor Tasik, founder of the metaverse advisory firm Meta Ventures, the concept that is inherent in the metaverse goes beyond the straightforward application of augmented reality (AR) and virtual reality (VR) technologies. In point of fact, Tasik argued in a recent interview that metaverse-inspired technology has the potential to become an ultimate experiential equaliser in the first half of the 21st century by integrating people's physical and digital existences in a hybrid virtual experience. This would occur as a result of the technology's ability to create a hybrid virtual experience.

According to a report published on bitcoin.com, one of the most prominent investment banks in the world, Morgan Stanley, believes that the metaverse and all of the products that are associated with it are poised to become the next major buzz concept in the world of investing.

The process of dematerializing

The 20th century was also a witness to another powerful force that would impact the global monetary and financial system, which up until that point had been based on material information stores like paper. This force was the introduction of a digital information storage system known as the blockchain. We are referring, of course, to the technological revolution that occurred during the era of computing, in which records and functions of many different kinds moved to digital drives made of silicon chips and transferred electronically. The process is referred to as "dematerialization" in the context of financial assets (which literally means exchanging a paper certificate for a digital record). A comparable process in cash ultimately led to the internet of today, where paper currency accounts for only around 25% of consumer usage in the United States.

The advantages of storing data in smaller spaces and transmitting it at the speed of light did not, however, address every inefficiency that existed within the system. In point of fact, it brought to light the need to simultaneously satisfy jurisdictional requirements as money moved across borders, as well as the technological metric of interoperability, which refers to the capacity of systems built on distinct database architectures and programming languages to interact with one another.

In 1973, a society known as SWIFT (which stands for "Society for Worldwide Interbank Financial Telecommunication") was founded with the intention of acting as a common communication protocol that bridged the gap between various technological and jurisdictional barriers and boundaries. After going live in 1977, SWIFT's platform "... quickly became the reliable, trusted global partner for institutions all over the world," according to SWIFT. A messaging platform, a computer system that validated and routed messages, and a set of message standards were the primary components of the initial services. The standards were developed to enable a common understanding of the data across linguistic and system boundaries, as well as to enable the seamless, automated transmission, receipt, and processing of communications that are exchanged between users.

Making Money In The Metaverse And How To Do It

The Metaverse is a world that exists solely online; it is a virtual location that users can visit and explore. You can access it through a screen or by donning a virtual reality headset, whichever you prefer.

Invest in some real estate in the Metaverse.

Purchasing virtual land is the most effective method available for turning a profit in the Metaverse. The land is typically sold in the form of a non-fungible token (NFT), and the market leader or at least the most well-known company in the field of buying land in the Metaverse is known as Decentraland. In decentraland, you are able to purchase virtual land.

To find out more, visit www.decentraland.org.

If you go to the "marketplace," you will be able to find anything there.

You might want to check out some other websites, such as Sandbox, Axie Infinity, Illivium, or Roblox.

You could also go to www.metaverse.properties, which is the first company of its kind to specialise in virtual real estate.

When you go to their website and select 'invest,' you will see that they have a metaverse REIT. A Real Estate Investment Trust, also known as a REIT, is an organisation that was created to invest in real estate and distribute profits to its shareholders. Getting a return on your investment in this venture is as easy as buying something and then trying to resell it at a higher price. You can also construct your own home on it, advertise your own business on it, advertise for the business of another person, or rent it out as a space for advertising. The plan is to first purchase it, then try to make some money off of it in the interim, and finally sell it for a higher price than you paid for it.

In order to purchase a piece of real estate in Decentraland, you will need to have some MANA on hand. The MANA token serves as the underlying cryptocurrency for the platform known as Decentraland. The token for SandBox is referred to as SAND, while the token for Axie Infinity is written as AXS, and the token for Illuvium is written as ILV.

Tokens of the Metaverse

You have the option of purchasing the token that is associated with a particular Metaverse rather than actual property in that Metaverse. Let's say you believe one of the metaverses will soon become extinct, but you don't want to invest in real estate there because you find it too much of a hassle or you simply can't afford it. In that case, you have the option of purchasing metaverse tokens and obtaining a similar upside, provided that the Metaverse continues to perform well over the course of time.

MANA, SAND, AXS, and ILV are the four distinct options that are available right now. This would be very comparable to purchasing a share of stock; however, in this case, you are purchasing the coin or token that is associated with the Metaverse in question.

Index of the Metaverse

There is something known as the metaverse index that you can use instead of buying individual coins or tokens if you do not wish to do so. The metaverse index stores a variety of the many different tokens that are used in the metaverse. The image that follows provides a list of all of the different tokens that are currently being stored within this index.

143

When you purchase this index, you are actually purchasing the complete set of all of the tokens that are included in the index. When you purchase the Metaverse Index (MVI), you will receive a proportionately smaller amount of each of these individual cryptocurrencies. In the present moment, the largest allocation is held in ILV, followed by AXS, and then MANA. If you invest in the index, rather than picking a single Metaverse that you believe will be successful, you will receive a diverse selection of almost all of them. This presents a one-of-a-kind opportunity that should not be missed.

Taking Care Of The Garden

The next activity that you can experiment with is weeding gardens. This is not merely a means to increase one's financial standing. Spending some time in the open air, soaking up some rays of sunshine, breathing in some crisp air, and getting your muscles moving are all excellent activities to partake in. You don't just need to do this for your own home; you can also ask your parents to put in a good word to your neighbours, and you can schedule days of the week (especially during the holiday season) when you can visit your neighbours' homes and help them with their gardens!

The process of gardening requires careful preparation and planning at each step. Let's look at each one of them in turn, shall we?

●First thing to keep in mind is that weeds will always be present in gardens, and some of them will even produce seeds. There is a chance that applying pesticides to the soil in your garden to get rid of the weeds is not the healthiest option. There are a few ways to get rid of weeds, including pulling them out by hand, using a good garden hoe, or both.

Allowing chickens access to the garden can also be beneficial because they can help with weeding and scraping the soil. Tilling the soil is an additional successful strategy for weed control in gardens.

You should charge ten dollars for participating in this activity.

Pruning is an essential step in the cleaning process for a garden, and you need to remove any dead branches from the plant before you start cutting. It is a good idea to prune trees and shrubs in the winter because they are more visible at this time of year, which makes it simpler to assess the results of your work.

In addition, you should routinely remove dead leaves from your plants in order to maintain their impression of youth.

This is not an easy task! Put ten dollars down as the price for this service!

Pots and leaves have a tendency to amass a great deal of dust, and muck clings to them. Regularly cleaning them with a soft cloth, particularly the leaves, is a great way to deal with this issue. Pots and planters can be cleaned by washing them or scrubbing them with a towel. Leaves, despite the appearance that they are tough, are frequently quite delicate.

Put five dollars on the table for this.

It's a well-known fact that outdoor furniture will gather a significant amount of grime and dust over the course of a year. If they are extremely filthy, wash them with a hose; otherwise, keep them clean by wiping them down once a week with a damp towel. If they are extremely filthy, wash them with a hose. You should either fix or replace any garden furniture that is damaged or torn, as this detracts from the overall appearance of the garden.

If you want to replace the furniture that is in your neighbor's garden, you should first take an inventory of what is broken and worn out, and then discuss the matter with your neighbour. They might really appreciate your suggestions!

It will cost ten dollars to participate in this activity.Last but not least, if your garden or the garden of your neighbour is enclosed by glass doors and railings, washing them down is an essential task during the process of cleaning the garden. Over time, dust, dirt, and fingerprints will accumulate on glass, which will detract from the overall aesthetic of your yard and the rest of your home.

You should be able to get a spotless clean glass screen that complements your landscape by using window cleaner and a cloth without lint. This will require some effort on your part. Your yard will give the impression of being much cleaner if you wipe down the railings with a damp cloth. Railings are notorious for collecting dust.

Because of the amount of time and patience that will be required, the price for this will be twenty dollars.

Do you have any idea how much money you could potentially make if you were to clean the garden of someone else and do a good job of it? Earnings to the tune of seventy dollars are contained in there! Therefore, discuss the matter with your parents and devise an appropriate schedule for cleaning the garden, and then go make some money that you have worked for and will value for the rest of your life.

Sponsors and backers

When you hear the word "promoter," your mind most likely immediately goes to the person or organisation that advertises or draws attention to a particular sporting or entertainment event. Promoters are also present in the world of investments and operate in a manner that is analogous to that described above. Their objective is to raise capital in order to participate in a specific investment activity. These promoters actively seek out individuals who may be interested in investing and then bring information to those individuals regarding specific investments. Their ultimate goal is to locate capital that can be directed towards the investment opportunity that they are promoting before it is diverted to another location. They will receive a greater number of benefits in proportion to the amount of capital they bring in.

You should be familiar with the many distinct varieties of promoters that are out there.

Penny stock promoters are individuals or entities that are in the business of promoting the penny stock market, which is comprised of smaller businesses with shares that are priced at a lower price. These promoters might be individuals who are willing to provide positive testimonials in order to generate more interest in a specific investment. This will result in an increase in revenue as well as an increase in the value of the company's shares.

A government-based trade promoter is an entity that provides assistance to US companies in the process of promoting their goods or services in international markets.

Customers or clients of a company who have a positive interaction with that company and are happy to recommend it to others are examples of "casual promoters." The public will then hear about their positive experience from them, which may result in an increase in the number of customers and possible investors.

Someone who is trustworthy and who will provide you with reliable information in good faith is called an honest promoter. When dishonest promoters present investors with a distorted image of an investment opportunity, problems can arise. They may choose to conceal information on purpose in order to give the impression that the opportunity is without risk. Due to the prevalence of major scams, many promoters have been associated with criminal activity.

If you want to be successful as an investor, you need to learn how to conduct your own research and not let promoters completely sway your opinion in either direction. The amount of capital that these individuals are able to bring in is also a factor in their financial interest in the venture. Take into account the possibility that they are more concerned with protecting their own interests than yours. You should listen to what they have to say, but you shouldn't take what they say as the word of God. The fact that a promoter brings your attention to an opportunity that you might not have been aware of otherwise is the most significant benefit that they can provide for you as a customer. You are able to conduct your own research from this vantage point.

Bitcoin (BTC) The Lightning Network, SegWit Innovations based on Networks

Scalability has consistently been Bitcoin's most pressing technical challenge since the cryptocurrency was first introduced. To put it another way, Bitcoin's ability to process a growing number of transactions in the real world. The time it takes to process a transaction on the Bitcoin network is currently 10 minutes, although this time could increase during times of high demand. As a result, this is beneficial to banks and other major financial institutions because a processing time of 10 minutes is significantly faster than that of SWIFT and other payment networks. A payment time of ten minutes is simply too lengthy and inefficient for smaller businesses such as a coffee shop, which is why these businesses are unable to afford it.

For years, there has been much debate regarding the strategy that would most effectively increase the size of Bitcoin's blocks. The longer these debates go on, the more challenging it will be to come up with any solutions that are actually viable. There are those who favour a hard fork, which loosens the restrictions imposed by the protocol, and there are those who favour a soft fork, which strictly adheres to the regulations imposed by the protocol.

Users who are in favour of a soft fork have proposed a mechanism that is known as Segregated Witness, or SegWit, without delving too deeply into the extensive technical particulars. Because SegWit allows for the signature (or witness) of a transaction to be kept separate from the data of the transaction, it is possible for more blocks to be created, which in turn enables more transactions to be processed. Because the witness information is encoded and cannot be

158

altered, the information that is associated with the sender of the payment cannot be modified. Numerous applications in the real world can be found for this, particularly in terms of lowering the risk that a transaction will be hacked.

Any potential shift is accompanied by a certain amount of unpredictability on its own. However, at the time of writing, SegWit has been active for less than 72 hours, and the price has remained the same so far. In actuality, the activation of SegWit will affect the value of Bitcoin in some way or another in the very near future.

It's possible that the implementation of SegWit would throw open the door to the lightning network, which will make it possible to conduct Bitcoin transactions at the speed of light. As was mentioned earlier, instant transactions will be of great assistance to micro and nano transactions. This will make it possible for smaller businesses to reap the benefits of accepting Bitcoin payments through point-of-sale terminals, which was not previously possible. This will be of particularly great benefit in locations where the value of the local fiat currency is low. In comparison to the value of the US dollar, the value of the Venezuelan bolivar has dropped by more than 90 percent in just under a year.

Transactions based on Bitcoin are providing assistance to a relatively small but sizable portion of Venezuela's population in maintaining the purchasing power of the money they do possess.

Capitalised Assets

On a balance sheet, fixed assets are denoted by the abbreviation "PP&E," which stands for "property, plant, and equipment." These are physically set in stone and consist of the land, machinery, buildings, fixtures, technology, and other assets that are owned by the company and contribute to productivity. They are an asset. Depending on the sector in which you work, this item may go by a different name. It is more likely that they will have distribution centres rather than plants for their retail stores.

You need an understanding of depreciation in order to appreciate the worth of property, plant, and equipment. Accountants take into account natural wear and tear, as well as technological obsolescence, by deducting depreciation from the purchase price of assets on a yearly basis. This practise is known as "depreciation." The decision of whether or not to undervalue the cost or the market value is another significant aspect to consider.

The value of the property, plant, and equipment (PP&E) will vary depending on the location of the firm, the nature of the equipment, and the manner in which it is operated. Obviously, all of these things are unique to their respective industries. Land is the one piece of property, plant, and equipment that is not affected by depreciation charges since land continues to increase in value over time. Unless there are a significant number of lands, investors will typically provide valuations that are on the more conservative side when it comes to the PP&E. They never value anything higher than fifty percent.

The Value of a Falling Asset and its Appreciation

The value of a PP&E asset is reduced through the process of depreciation in a methodical manner, and then a corresponding sum of money is assigned to a period expense, which is an expense that has been documented over a predetermined reporting period. The price that a company paid for an item is not the only thing that is recorded in its books. Instead, they choose an approach known as depreciation, which involves spreading out the cost of ownership over a number of years. After the depreciation cycle has run its course, the company will make a fresh capital expenditure, acquire a new asset to replace the one that was depreciated, and then restart the cycle from the beginning.

When it comes to the assignment of depreciation dollars, there are just two primary categories of methodologies that you need to be familiar with in order for this book to accomplish its goals and stay within its scope:

• The method of straight-line depreciation, in which an equal amount of the asset's worth is written off each year until the asset's value reaches zero;
• The method of accelerated

depreciation, in which the amount written off in the initial years of the asset is proportionately larger than it was in later years. One of these approaches is called the "double declining balance," while another is called the "sum of the years' digits."

The method of depreciation that was chosen is important. Because accelerated depreciation requires conservative assessments of property, plant, and equipment (PP&E), as well as earnings, this leaves even more room in the future for prospective growth in net earnings, because it is safe to assume that the majority of the depreciation has already occurred. However, there are businesses out there that opt to use tactics that are straight-line in order to make it appear as though their present earnings are significantly more than they actually are. Be on the watch for businesses that make the transition from accelerated procedures to straight-line ways.

Make Sure The Storage Is Done Right

Wallets designed for use with cryptocurrencies such as bitcoin offer users an extremely secure location in which to store their virtual assets. You are the only one who should have access to the private key to your cryptocurrency funds if you are able to store them in your own wallet rather than letting them circulate in the trading community. In addition to this, it gives you the option to keep your funds in cold storage, which lowers the likelihood that your cryptocurrency exchange will be hacked and that you will lose any assets you have stored there.

Some wallets are more expensive than others, and some offer a greater number of features than others. While others offer the opportunity to purchase for a variety of different crypto currencies, some are solely focused on Bitcoin transactions.

A useful function that is included in certain wallets is the ability to exchange one token for another. When deciding on a wallet for your Bitcoins, you have a number of different options available to you to pick from.

To get started, you need to be aware that there are two different types of cryptocurrency wallets, which are referred to as hot wallets (wallets that are stored online) and cold wallets (wallets that are stored offline) (paper or hardware wallets).

Cash on the Table

Wallets that are stored online are frequently referred to as "hot" wallets. Some examples of internet-connected gadgets that are capable of operating as hot wallets include computer systems, mobile phones, and capsules.

Because digital wallets generate the private keys to your currencies on devices that are linked to the internet, the security of your financial assets may be compromised as a consequence.

When you store your private key on a device that is connected to the internet, the security of that key is compromised, making it more likely that it will be stolen. Hot pockets, on the other hand, are incredibly convenient because they permit you to quickly access and transact with your possessions.

When using such hot wallets, users who do not take adequate precautions to protect their financial information run the risk of having their price range stolen from right under their eyes. This possibility may also appear implausible.

This does not necessarily constitute an exceptional event, and it is possible for it to take place in a wide variety of contexts and methods.

It would not be wise, for instance, to boast on a public discussion board such as Reedit about how amazing of a deal you had on Bit Coin while simultaneously using a system with very little to no protection and carrying it around in a hot pocket.

Having said that, it is feasible to make these wallets more relaxed so long as necessary safeguards are maintained. Minimum criteria such as strong passwords, two-factor authentication, and secure internet browsing should be taken into consideration.

If you only have a small quantity of Bitcoin or if you frequently buy and sell cryptocurrency on an exchange, one of these wallets is the best option for you. If we were to compare it to a bank account, it would be the most efficient option. Keeping the money that is most easily accessible for spending in a bank account is one of the more common pieces of traditional financial advice. The remainder of your funds should be put in savings, debt, or other forms of finance.

The exact same thing can be said with hot wallets, in case you were wondering about its applicability.

Computers, mobile devices, the internet, and online trading accounts "Hot wallets" is a catch-all phrase that encompasses all types of custodial wallets. As was said before, change wallets are essentially custodial accounts that are provided by the alternative payment processor.

There is a good chance that the person who uses this wallet is not the same person who possesses the private key to the bitcoins that are stored in it.

In the event that the exchange is hacked or your account is compromised, you run the risk of having all of your money stolen. On crypto currency discussion boards and in crypto currency groups, it is a phrase that is frequently repeated, "you no longer have your key, and you no longer have your coin."

Freezing Wallets

A pocket that is not linked to the internet and, as a consequence, is at a greatly decreased risk of being hacked is referred to as a cold wallet. This is the simplest way to characterise what is known as a cold wallet. In certain circles, these wallets are also referred to as offline wallets or hardware wallets. Other names for them include cold storage wallets. A person's private key is kept on anything that is not linked to the internet, and these wallets may include a software application that functions in parallel with the wallet to enable the user to check their portfolio without putting the privacy of their private key at risk.

Keep a Good Mood and a Positive Attitude.

Holocaust survivor, nervous system expert, and author of "Man's Search for Meaning" Victor Frankel once said, "Everything can be taken from a man except for a certain something: the remainder of the human opportunities— to choose one's mentality in some random situation, to choose one's own particular manner." Frankel is known for his book "Man's Search for Meaning." His choice of demeanour was critical to his ability to survive the horrible treatment he received in Auschwitz, which took place in Poland under Nazi occupation during World War II.

The mindset that one has also has a significant role in one's level of success and abundance. In many cases, it is given a higher importance than previous experience or available resources. The correct frame of mind is one that engages in "plausibility thinking" rather than critical and incredulous thinking. The way in which we interpret the world around us is not always set in stone.

If I just "think positive," an issue won't magically go away no matter how I look at it, contrary to what logical experts have said me in the past, so stop fooling yourself into thinking that it will. I couldn't agree with you more. To put it another way, positive reasoning won't cure a disease, make you a scratch golfer, or make up for a negative balance in your bank account, and that's exactly the idea. You need to zero down on the problem at hand and find a solution.

You have the option of viewing it as either a potential opportunity or a potential hindrance to your progress. In any event, it is still there, but if you approach the test with a positive attitude, it will end up being an essential instructor rather than an exercise in futility and assets. This is provided, of course, that you approach the test with a positive attitude. The decision is entirely up to us, and we have unrestricted discretion over how we understand any given set of circumstances.

— — — — — — —

It is not the circumstances themselves that determine one's attitude, but rather how one interprets the events occurring around them.

— — — — — — —

There is a tale that goes somewhat like this: A British shoe manufacturer dispatched two sales representatives to Africa many years ago in order to investigate the continent's prospective consumer base. The top sales representative went back to the office perplexed and dejected, then declared, "There is no potential here—no one wears shoes." The subsequent sales representative surged into the meeting room, overflowing over with enthusiasm, and yelled, "There is gigantic potential here—no one has shoes!" It's all about how you look at things.

To put this into a modern context, you have the option of how to react in the event that a medical treatment case is postponed or a consumer does not show up for an appointment. You have two options: one is to complain about the situation, and the other is to look at it as an opportunity to accomplish other work, make up for missed time with your reading, or call to check in on a relative. In any event, the situation won't develop in a different way.

The author of Chicken Soup for the Soul, Mark Victor Hansen, is quoted as saying, "It's your perspective, not your conditions, that decides if it will be a decent day or an awful day." It is not the circumstances themselves that determine one's attitude, but rather how one interprets the events occurring around them. If you have to choose between being annoyed and angry or relieved and regaining some of your energy, go with the latter option.

The people you attract to your primary objective will be partially determined by your attitude. You have the choice of working with positive masterminds who regularly remove obstacles, or you can work with negative scholars who are unable to see past the problems. Maintain a confident and upbeat attitude at all times. You'll amass wealth far more quickly, and the journey there will be a lot more cnjoyable.

New Viewpoints That Will Completely Change The Way You Think The Third The Influence That Passive Income Can Have

This is the point where everything starts to get interesting on its own.

One definition of "automated revenue" is "pay that does not require you to work for it." You might hear people refer to it as money that you can make while you're sleeping every once in a while. In spite of the fact that this is completely evident, there is still some uncertainty around simple sources of income. Some people understand this to suggest that they won't have to perform any work in exchange for the promised income, which is an interpretation that is rarely justified. To generate revenue using automated means can require a significant level of activity front and centre, such as searching for knowledge and training oneself to be able to make use of automated revenue generation options. In addition, once you begin to get automated money, there is typically some maintenance work that you will need to perform in order to ensure that the automated revenue continues to flow.

For instance, you have an investment property and hire a property director to handle the various responsibilities associated with being a landlord on your behalf. The income from that investment property will continue to come in, and you won't need to deal directly with the tenants or the restrooms on a regular basis in order to collect it. However, if you let years pass without monitoring the property manager and you only occasionally redesign the building, the pay will most likely stop at some point in the future. This is especially likely if you occasionally change the building. In spite of the fact that you are not practically required for the payment to be made, you will still end up making money during your downtime, but this does not mean that you will never have to put in any effort towards the investment.

However, apart from the initial setup and ongoing maintenance of the source of money, automated revenue allows you to collect pay even while you are sleeping. That's the secret: even when you're not putting in any effort, money keeps coming in. This opens the door to a certain degree of opportunity that most people are unaware of.

What would it be like for a person to go about their daily life if they were able to derive all of their income from sources that did not require their physical presence in order to process payments or transactions? Indeed, it can give the appearance of anything they want it to if they want it to. Give it some thought. How long have you had this responsibility, and how does it interact with the work that you undertake every day? It's not only the fact that you work more than 40 hours a week that keeps you from moving forward. Include the time it takes to get to and from work in those daily hours. In a similar vein, remember to include in time for preparation and decompression. This refers to the time you spend getting ready for work and the time you spend recovering from it after you get home. The location of your place of employment is a crucial factor in determining where you should make your home. You are limited in where you can reside unless you are able to work from home, so you should choose a location that is relatively close to your place of employment. Consider that you are required to commit anywhere from ten to fourteen hours of each day to your job in some capacity, and that you are also restricted to living in a particular location.

If you don't enjoy what you do for a living and you don't like where you live, it's hard to know how much you're missing out on in your day-to-day existence. You have little energy for anything else during the week other from your job, and because of it, you won't be able to experience many things that you enjoy because your employment ties you down to a particular location.

If we take away the work, what does this thing look like? Imagine for a moment that you actually had an amount of simple revenue that was capable of supporting your lifestyle to the point where you didn't need to work under any circumstances. If you didn't have to spend 10 to 14 hours a day working because of the fact that you live so far away from the activities that you enjoy, what would a typical day look like for you?

The answer is "retirement."

Consider the actions that people take when they decide to quit their jobs. They don't need to be up at a specific time, they can relax the entire day if they want to, they can make a trip whenever they want to, they can go visit loved ones whenever they want to, and they try to do all of the things that they've long wanted to do but never had the opportunity to do while they were working. They don't need to be up at a specific time.

In the case that none of your money was processed, this is the course of action that you would be given the opportunity to take. When you don't need to be at a specific job at a given time, you don't need to be at a specific employment, and this gives you the option to schedule your days exactly how you want them to be, you are experiencing lifestyle design.

Principal Constituents

The following three components are required for any excellent strategy to function properly, regardless of the form of the strategy. These constituents are undeniably present at all times. Because of this, you cannot afford to disregard them. Should you choose to ignore them, they will eventually turn around and bite you. Therefore, it is in your best interest to deal with them as soon as possible. If you do so, you will be able to avoid a wide variety of problems in the future.

A State of Liquidity

The ease with which you would be able to buy and sell an asset is referred to as its liquidity. While certain assets have a high degree of liquidity, others do not. The ease with which one could sell something, particularly during times of instability, is what this term refers to. An excellent illustration of an illiquid asset is a piece of real estate, for instance. After all, you can't expect to sell a house in only five minutes even if you try your hardest. It could take you a few weeks or even a few months before you receive a favourable offer.

Assets with a high degree of liquidity include commodities (gold, oil), currencies, and attractive stocks (blue-chip corporations such as Apple, Facebook, or GM). It is possible that you already have offers lined up for the asset, but this would depend on the type of the asset. Therefore, make sure you put most of your attention on liquid assets.

On the other hand, although illiquid assets could generate high profits, it might be difficult to sell them when the market is in a downturn. Real estate, intellectual property, and industrial assets are all examples of things that are valuable but have a difficult time finding purchasers. When compared to strategies focused on the short term, buy-and-hold investing in these assets is the superior choice.

The risk of fluctuation

The quantity of trade volume that is taking place at any given point is referred to as volatility. For instance,

189

volatility tends to increase first thing in the morning when trading begins. This is an unavoidable consequence that arises as a direct result of the participation of each and every player in the game.

Another factor that can contribute to an increase in volatility is the occurrence of unanticipated events in the economy. These occurrences may take the shape of weak economic data, policies enacted by the government, or natural disasters. On the other hand, these occurrences might also have a good outcome. In the case that they are favourable developments, there may be an increase in volatility in the form of buying rather than selling.

It is possible that you will not have the opportunity to generate substantial gains while volatility is low. As a result, an HFT strategy is the most effective.

When market volatility is strong, it's possible that undervalued companies will surprise everyone and outperform their peers. Therefore, it is advisable to look for firms that are inexpensive before volatility increases. Then, as the level of volatility grows, you will be able to sell amidst the commotion.

Volume

The term "volume" refers to the total number of times a particular individual has been traded during a given period of time. The volume of a stock's trading activity is one factor that determines how liquid it is. As a result, the stock's lack of popularity might be inferred from the low volume. As a consequence of this, you can have a hard time selling it within a short period of time. On the other hand, if a stock has a high trading volume, you can buy and sell it with complete self-assurance whenever your circumstances require it. When analysing a single stock for high-frequency trading, this is the most important sign that you should look at.

www.ingramcontent.com/pod-product-compliance
Lightning Source LLC
Chambersburg PA
CBHW071215210326
41597CB00016B/1819